DECLARATION FOR YOUR BONES

DECLARATION FOR YOUR BONES

Duane Esposito

For Nicholas,

For poetry + the
salt depth of
mystery.   4/8/13

Yuganta Press

Yuganta Press
6 Rushmore Circle
Stamford, CT 06905-1029
ralphnazareth@mac.com

For Lisa, Genevieve, & Joseph

For none ever self-destructs,
no matter how abandoned,
& those who menace us
are Gods now unemployed.

— *Rainer Maria Rilke,* from *Orchards*

Contents

A Note to the Reader

The book you hold in your hands fell into mine in manu-
script form at a time when terrifying anxiety had be-
come my constant companion. A few months earlier my
wife, my partner of almost four decades, the mother of
our children and the better half of Yuganta Press, had
been diagnosed with stage 4 cancer, and our world was
cracked at the foundations.

Duane Esposito's poems, relentless in their open-
ness to pain and fierce in their defense of the life of lan-
guage, promised dark consolation. Mingling with the
shadows in my life, they became part of the prayerful
attention that charged my waking moments. It was not
before I endured the passing away of my dear wife and
gave mute witness to dire world events, including the
carnage in Iraq and the hanging of Saddam, that I un-
dertook to publish them.

The following excerpts from my letters to the author

will, I hope, give you not only a glimpse of the evolution of my response to his work — and it is only one reader's response — but also afford you an insight into what happens when author and publisher step across professional lines to enter a space where poetry invites us to walk hand in hand.

2/6/07

I read *Declaration*... in one sitting as it drew me irresistibly into its core of pain and heart of light. If poetry is therapeutic, it must be so not because it makes one feel better or lighter or more hopeful about oneself and the world, but because it helps with the cure of the disease we may not be quite aware of, viz. our inattention to life, to what's before us, behind us, within us. Therapy stems from a deeper knowing entwined with the grip of pain — one's own as well as that of the "tears in things."

...Thank you for your profound gift — of self, of word, of self and other worlds. I'm not sure when Linda will read it, but I will certainly share your beautiful handwritten letter with her. Now that we're past the electric athleticism of surgery, a sudden pall shadows us, and it grieves me to see her once again slip into a cycle of withdrawal. I don't know what's in store for us, but with the love and caring of friends we know we'll refuse to let meaning die before the end.

I'm writing these few words through the fog of exhaustion. Linda and I are due to be at Sloan tomorrow and again on Friday. I don't know how she endures this. She must love us all deeply.

I manage to stay focused on the immediate. But I feel a strong undertow of the absurd — in being connected to Linda's pain and the universal transience it underscores while unable to dismiss the sun's faithfulness and the durability of things.

11/10/08

I've just read your latest *Declaration*.... I'm not sure what I'm doing responding in words. I must become silent in its presence. Maybe I have become so at a level I don't quite apprehend. With this partial assurance I move forward in words (how else?) to say how deeply it touches me — as it did in its first version.

I read it now *post mortem*. I read it in Linda's absence. I read it among the ashen residue of her bones. Yet nothing I feel or know replicates your pain. It can't. Yet again, if your poetry, or anyone else's, should speak to me in ways that do more than merely pique my curiosity and interest, do more than merely remind me that I'm part of a universe of discourse, if it should wake me up in a way that makes returning to ordinary time and sleep impossible, it must then create in me the same "blue" or "inky songs" that haunt and blow through your lines, so stripped down yet bulging with sentience and the hope that lives in the knowing of desperation. This is the only way for us, it seems to me — that we write to find an echo that bubbles up from a level below the water-glass image of Narcissus, that we write without the vain effort to move beyond, that we huddle wrapped in the given, the impossible present. You do this. And thus give me a gift.

But that is not all.

4/11/09

...Your poems, the cry of desolation and connection in abandonment..., especially on this Good Friday.

I've just come back from a service in which the priest tried to dissociate the cross from the "twisted logic of appeasing a cruel God" (à la the Aztecs,) and his assistant said, "We do not celebrate Good Friday," but then after a long pause added, "but we hunger." So true, so devastatingly true....

(These reflections) hold a line that you and I have been following, I believe, and are bound to for a long time, since there's very little else worth thinking about except the breakthrough in the breakdown.

4/28/09

...I am consoled by the thought that I don't need to say anything now for a while since you have delved into the complexity of the braided or tangled connections among word, words, faith, imagination, the seen and the unseen.... We're discovering something together even in the act of rehearsing a lot of what we know already and hold to be true or know only imperfectly and in "hints and guesses."

...my loss of Linda is very much with me, the sadness, the regrets...coming at me in waves. All I can do is pay attention.

Yuganta may be the dwelling for your ...*Bones*. Perhaps you'll be done with the ms. in spring. ...I know you to be a poet who doesn't rush to produce and publish. I respect and admire your commitment to the craft and vision both of us consider central to our lives.

Your meditation has pulsed in my folder. I've entered its movement and stayed there in deep sympathy. It seems impossible to invite enough people into this process of reflection for it to make a difference. I can almost feel the giant wheels of entropy grinding away slowly, invisibly. I'll leave it there for now — a dark note.

A common cold has stopped me from driving down to my brother's in Va. for the celebration of an incipient marriage alliance, the start of yet another germinal cycle. So I turn to *Declaration*... one more time. Among my loved ones, I'd have been embraced with joy and laughter; here in this book I am engulfed by a scream. For that is what *Declaration*... is — in part and whole.

I think again of Icarus. Is there any time I don't? Tragic flaw or not, he plunges, and plunges for ever, it seems. But who cares? We do not have time, as Auden's old masters teach us, for revelations. My friend who told me, "When dad died, I took a lunch break, then went back to work," speaks for us all. We have work to do.

But wait. Do we not also deeply sense that every cry at the sheer pain and sameness of our ordinary lives on this ever-dying and nauseatingly resurgent planet, every "tear in the widow's eye," is an exhortation, however agonizing? A scream is an *azaan*, a call to prayer, a call to life. So it is as a publisher releasing *Declaration for Your Bones*, I indulge in my favorite desperate act, calling those who form my little world: Come, drink. It's bitter. But it's good.

Ralph Nazareth

faith is what is
important.

on line 14 he makes a
Direct address... breaks into
logic if... Then, two sides to
a coin.

Vacancy

We're a skull that cannot close
around a brain of light —

a marriage connection — two thin,
ribbed chests pressed against each other.

We stare at veins around eyes,
foreign to our lives,

blind to the moon in early morning,
blind to prayers & questions.

There isn't a hand God will extend.
He loves His doldrums — leans inside us,

& we can't clarify the difference
between absence & infinity.

We try & we try.
The failure that is yours.

This way.
The failure might be mine.

That way.
Lightning goes two ways.

Handwritten annotations:

What is a skull that cannot close?

IT cannot contain our light our soul our essence

Runs — no closure.

we are awkward — maybe ugly in our physical form

We do not recognize ourselves in others ... skulls are only capable of staring. only surface details do we observe the heavens are beyond

almost as if we were given our form so that we can feel pain

because we fail to hold the light we are unable to see too — we are not alone and so solitude is our existence — becomes

Middle

|4|

?

Royal "US"
We are alone... hard to be alone
and said,

Us & no one else:
the saddest work of all.

PUPPETS
Actors on stage

not
for
but
in

At best, our ministrations
toward one another are dead.

we are lifeless
just going
through
motions

The
Direction
of

We insist on declaration, & every faith,
every crisis, every word is fiction.

faith has been reduced
To declaration ... makes us prone
To exaggeration ...Do we need
To lie to make ourselves
interesting?

Limbo & The Rain

These days, being here is just another day,
& most things seem a little low & sad.

A voice is all we have to reconcile history,
but there's little song.

Do you feel, like I do,
the panic that disfigures?

Do you know, like I do,
love cannot survive?

These days, being here is just another day,
& most things seem a little low & sad.

The blank, blank, blank.
It's love's scattered wound.

It's end of winter snow,
blue humiliation, the new moon.

Do you feel, like I do,
the panic that disfigures?

Do you know, like I do,
love cannot survive?

A pin stuck into the skin
insists attention.

Limbo's not the birds —
they don't make our sadness.

Heaven's not the one dove
heard beyond the rain.

These cries, these inky
songs, belong to limbo.

It's a kind of dying, less a melody
& more the act of singing.

Around Here

The day burns —
a blue, almost flame.

It's cold, the view's
only gray, & it breaks me.

There's too much time, too many hours.
I've had too much to think.

I have no idea what others
see when they look at me.

Even angels, the hopeful echoes,
are north of where they're needed.

Time won't kick away sadness.
It's so dark in here I can't find the sky.

Tell me, please, is love
recovery or a blast of light?

Proximity or distance?
What's the difference?

As I get near my wounds,
there's hardly room to know.

Love's enough questioning.
The void blasts & shatters.

I lean toward its sounds, wait for reply:
is it wind that visits nowhere?

Skinny Daddy

(for my daughter, Genevieve)

Alarmed by a razor,
I pick it up & cut my flesh,
white as the moon, white as damage.

It's pornographic — quick & ugly —
impossible violence in discrete locations.
It does harm love, & I embrace an old news,

horizons I cannot see, the absence of touch.
& the night comes loose. I don't go
hunting the untouched winter.

I've swallowed the history of losing half my body,
of going to sleep a whole child & waking as a half.
It's the numbness of coma.

Because I — most of all — have no idea
what others see when they look
at me, at this body. What do you see?

Singular is an illusion,
a fiction made of ego,
& all anxiety is born of this distraction.

Sky

We insist death
won't soon arrive.

There never was a time
crows didn't sparkle.

If we fail to witness,
if we fail to wake,

we embody disease & believe
the distance between here & heaven.

Our light's gnawed on,
always a kind of dying.

Living's how we wonder
if there's bearing on the ground.

After death
we're dead — I guess.

But God knows everything
about peace & quiet:

no words, my love, only
the winter woods inside us.

Anniversary

Because we've only tried,
does love keep company
with the rest of our exiled needs?

I'm staring at the black beneath your eyes.
December's moon is above the unconscious.

It's criminal. The snow arrives.
& everything follows fury.

Much Explodes

This is my declaration for your bones:
grief is the deepest cold.

& the trees are spiny. & the wind numbs.
& the sky's unforgiving & blue.
& my body, too, goes down to the bones.

All of this, my love,
I've blamed on you —
down to your bones.

So much explodes.
I can't reconcile memory with love —
desire with the history of starving.

& then: about your eyes, or mine,
has anything here to do with love,
or the beast we'd like to threaten us?

& then: I'm the single, black cloud
hovering inside our home.
My God, I hate ceilings.

Is nearly dying your memory of starving?
Mine's the pins stuck into the skin.

Spring

We're witness to decay. We're dying of decay.
We state our rage. It has been ten years.

Little here has changed.
Tell me, Love, convince me of the spring.

You're trying, still, to get your weight
up from 102.

Mostly, when you speak
I don't listen.

You're trying, still, to stare at what it means
to long for solid bones.

Mostly, what I desire
you don't provide.

There isn't even a sky above the ocean —
no blue music to accompany our drowning.

Aren't we startled
& aren't we disfigured?

All these Decembers —
the nothing & the nowhere.

Maybe we need the deepening
of a common gash between us.

& I'm growing tired
of the time that's passing,

& you're embracing loneliness
as a necessary silence,

& here's another boredom
& another humiliation,

one more moment
& yet another hour,

another declaration
for yet another season.

Our already aching lives. Please
let us not leave each other.

Please,
let us not leave

our bones paling in the slant, spring sunlight
beside an empty garden, waiting for next year.

We must pray
& then arrive.

Waking is a dark time, a nearly abandoned station
between unidentified worlds.

Anyway

I'm a wide killing area.
Angels have cut the ropes
to my invisible heaven.

After all the years
I was going to fear
everything, anyway.

To Numb Love

It has something to do with drugs.
400 hits of acid, handfuls of Quaaludes,
mescaline, mushrooms, & ounces of weed.

That was those days.
Here are these:

Up & down, high & gone.
The reasons for the drugs I've taken.
The reasons for the drugs I take.

Reasons are rooted in ways
I'd rather not say. Would you?

Here Are The Days

Here's this memory:
the age of eight.

I nearly died from an explosion in my brain.
When does a lifetime begin to speak?

Here's this memory:
the age of fifteen.

I walked across the L.I.E. stoned on Quaaludes:
there goes September & the sky.

Here's this memory:
the age of seventeen.

My parents are divorced.
My childhood dog is dead.

My mother's boyfriend buys
the family a new dog.

& this one: I give that miniature poodle
a hit of white, blotter acid.

You see, I've refused to let anyone offer
what I'm unwilling to take.

These days, regardless of memory,
God's a stillness in me.

I haven't died.
Faith's a still voice.

I'm forty-five, & I fear death.
This is not a memory.

These are the days
that will carry me toward dying.

Sudden Rain

When I'm dying,
where will my mind be?

Is dying one kind of attention?
The birds outside my window are gone.

Why should I pray —
if God knows nothing about living?

I think my eyes are bleeding.
Do your eyes bleed in summer?

I don't care if it ever stops raining.
Maybe some other God knows something.

Crude

I'm in the examination room.
In walks the doc.
She's hot.
She has taken the time
to dress to accentuate her mid-age body —
tight & held together nice.

She asks me questions about my boy:
"Does he track you
when he sees you come into a room?"
"Does he babble?" "Does he drool?"
These are just a few. Then she asks,
"Do you have any questions for me?"

"Can I brush your hair every night before sleep?"
"Does your ass swing a little when you walk
to the can?" "Does your pot-belly jiggle
when you bounce real hard?" "Does God
only appear when our fantasies are gentle?"

I'm a man. I'm watching.
You look lovely, doc.
& one more question.
Sorry if it's crude.
"Is the smell down there as fantastic as you look?"

The Ghost of Pornography

There aren't any heroes.
I'll need another day.

Another day arrives.
I find another way

to discover I'm alone
& can't begin to say.

The hours drag on.
My tendons get stiff.

My eyes & my balls
& my fingertips itch.

Each obscene image fades love.
I hate the invisible.

It reminds me of bones —
the unnoticed Gods.

Anorexia, the ghost of pornography,
terrifies & efficiently haunts me.

Killing Field

All the words
we didn't say
& all the words
we did
are buried in
a lopsided killing field,
no longer ours.

It's About Living

& here. I'm alone too long
in the past inside of memory,
in the brain swollen by explosion,

in the body paralyzed by too much
rushing blood to the brain,
to the trauma, to the echo, to the pinpoint.

I nearly understand
how to stop time.
It can be found in the leap

between memory & now:
That day. This day.
Is living about time?

How fast is any day rushing?
Am I my memory? & here.
Is distortion of memory

what helps us survive?
Here. It's about living this day.
Here. It's about living another day.

& here, again.
I'm bored before I wake. I rise
like everyone has risen before.

Bones

The homunculus listens
to the brain inside my chest.

It hears this: no perfection
more perfect than a malformed body.

More & more it seems I'm dying.
To glow isn't anything without a source.

Then I see I've uttered
this description of our love —

a knotted, purple,
nameless, strange affliction,

the reality of bones:
the unnoticed Gods.

I push & push
& push toward Gods.

Dust & Blood

Although I must speak of grief —
of disgust & rage — I'm afraid,
these days, I've nothing to say.

You see, death undoes me:
to think of where I'll be
if not with those I love.

But, you see,
when marriage lacks sex,
lacks romance, has kids, kids we love

& who love us, do we?, we love each other,
a body grows to fit another body,
& we don't gaze much at trees,

golden & endearing, outside our high,
home window, which reminds me love ends.
&, then, I'm gone — I mean not here.

I wonder what pens
look like in heaven.

Here you are beside me —
arms folded across your chest —
& I rend memory, tear my throat out

thinking once again, the shock of witness,
the shock of awe: bin Laden's murder,
September's dust & blood.

It can't be, shouldn't be, is.
The rule of law, America,
broken before my eyes.

I won't be the same.
Grief doesn't end.
That way — this way.

Because of them.
Because of us, America.
Because of disgust & rage.

Once More In The Whitecaps Of Pain

So many others' loved ones are dead:
another famine, another poverty, another war.

Here's the depraved body politic:
who else matters but ourselves, our own?

Do I dare say human community, our family?
& do I dare drink whiskey, smoke some weed,
succumb to the numb, stoned general?

I mean, each time I wake I wake afraid —
reality, of course, isn't separate from pain —
of doubting love, yours & mine,
once more in the whitecaps of pain.

There are the ordinary birds. & just
as I watch them settle — sobering — they lift
from branches higher than the mind that dreamed
last night of mountains as places I could not go.

Where, now, are the ordinary birds,
& where's that one December hour we shared
while standing in the warmest rain?

Don't you see? Hope is our memory,
& memory makes comfort in the end.
What has God to do with me?

& what happened to my grave concern for others?
America's done.

Again & again — draft after draft —
I've tried to say a simple thing:
I'm lonely, & I'm tired of the pain.

I'd like to go down to the edge of some dark water
& walk until my face disappears into a sky without stars.

I'm losing time & doubting love.
This depression — yours & mine.

September

(for the families left behind)

Those nights when the cold's slow to settle,
the planet barely holds itself inside its own space.

The soul's roots grow stringy:
a certain moon, we chew September.

It echoes like a childhood fever,
& the mind tries to freeze the sky.

The odor of charred bodies
still lingers under ground.

May we ever have a month-long
memorial to grief?

September is the reason
for the sickness in our lives:

the faces of our loved ones
have blurred & disappeared.

Now to equal radiance
we pray to God.

We sit beside a field of purple flowers.
Love says hello again to something we believe.

There might be recovery.
There never is.

We can't think back before collapse.
Limbs were torn from bodies.

The bluest day.
Now pure abstraction.

God is miniscule.
It must be in the dust & blood.

When the hell is October
or any month but this one?

I think there's no cure for us —
if we want to go on living.

November

(for Anthony Piccione, 1939–2001)

This is the time when winter begins
& spring, it seems, will never arrive.
Because you're dead, old friend.

So listen. I'll tell you I'm the boy —
even though it's my mid-age —
who chews his bruises,

who can't reconcile love
with time, today
with the day I'll die.

Jameson & sleeping pills,
& I slog through nights
in search of motion
so as not to remain in place.

November is the month you died.
Where the hell is spring?
Perhaps the thing I'll remember is
only memory survives.

The Starving

The starving of those days,
it's disappeared from these days,
equals moontime — mine.

Imagine one crossing too many
as history God forgives & tell me, then,
where will we be when we're dead?

Does death mean leaving behind
the people we love?

Where might we find love?
Where sky is torn on concrete?

Where the hell is dawn,
the heel of night?

Even God — a word for witness —
is blind.

Memory, of course,
is the color of remorse,
especially as we live & dream.

The Belt

I know nearly nothing of my father.
He served his country in WW II.
Memory's a kind of shell shock.

Shell shock recalls stories never told.
Shell shock hangs on a railing.

How do I construct a memory
out of this memory of you?

Here: shell shock you whip me.
Generosity doesn't equal a man.

& here: shell shock you leave.
Absence is the memory of love.

You've been gone for thirty-eight years.
I'm afraid this fact is boring.

Most things hurt when we pay attention.
This is no exception.

The Loons

The rain falls steadily inside your head.
You will die quite cloistered by autistic music.

The leaves these days
drift toward home.

If you fail to fly,
they will murder your psyche.

Do you know dalliance
transforms God into a spook?

2

To close the distance between vast shores,
I cease being tired of memory.

To no longer chew the bruises of history,
I speak for the constancy of love.

To no longer wonder
what it means to be alive,

I refuse to be dragged
through infantile desires.

Here's the terror I've had to bury:
you left me with a paralyzed, half-body.

I announce my obsession with rain.
I'm sorry for the stardust that led to creation.

3

Sometimes, when clouds
touch water, you'll soon arrive.

I reach for you — my gone father —
for the blank you left behind.

But loons, once in the whitecaps of pain,
have left these lakes for winter.

In dream they sleep near my head
& twitch against my neck.

Echoes Of California

When we see the moon above a lake,
we never cry for long.

We witness a smaller planet,
our wild & physical world.

The sunrise is distance without confusion,
& it never fails our kisses,

or shade near lakes,
or loons in wind.

You see, I don't own your bones.
You gave them to me long ago —

on a floor beneath a blanket,
in the dark, alone — & I held them:

a solitary graveyard
on the other side of wilderness.

When lives choke evolving shapes,
especially as we think of God,

there's an alarming comprehension
of the failure of our choices,

& pain's constant as dreaming.
Don't you dream?

Can bones grow strong & beautiful?
All the angels are too thin for any common yielding.

Acknowledgments

There are too many people to thank: Lisa Esposito, Genevieve Esposito, Joseph Esposito, Brian Esposito, Dan Childress, Jay Auerfeld, Anthony Piccione (1939–2001), Jon Palzer, & Sheida Dayani. Each of you has helped me to live &, therefore, to write this poetry.

Thanks also to the Nassau Community College Sabbatical Committee & Board of Trustees for granting me a sabbatical during which portions of this book were completed.

& to the editors of the following publications where many of these poems, often in earlier versions, first appeared: *Chronogram; Church On Thursday; Global City Review; Jackson Heights Poetry Festival Online Library; Long Island Pulse; The Long Islander; Long Island Sounds Anthology; Poetic Conventions; Polarity; Toward Forgiveness Anthology; World Wide Word Radio Network.*

Thank you to Eva Ash & Mom for your close attention to many drafts.

Thank you to Gladys Henderson for your continued support of my work.

I especially thank Scott Ash, to whom I am indebted for

his thorough & precise reading of my work, which has made me a better writer & editor.

& to William Heyen: after so many years, you're still my teacher. For this I'm grateful.

Finally, thank you to Ralph Nazareth, a man of depth & purpose who cares for poetry & the soul. I'm honored to be an author with Yuganta Press.

About the Author

Duane Esposito is an Associate Professor of English at Nassau Community College in Garden City, New York. He has an M.A. from SUNY Brockport and an M.F.A. from the University of Arizona. In 1994, Diane Glancy selected his work for an Academy of American Poets Award. In 2003 & 2010, he was nominated for a Pushcart Prize. His poems have appeared in dozens of publications. *Declaration For Your Bones* (Yuganta Press, 2012) is his third book. Previously, he has published two books of poetry: *Cadillac Battleship* (brokenTribe Press, 2005), & *The Book of Bubba* (Brown Dog Press, 1998). He lives on Long Island with his wife & children.